CODING
WITH
SCRATCH

Coding with Basher ™

CODING WITH SCRATCH

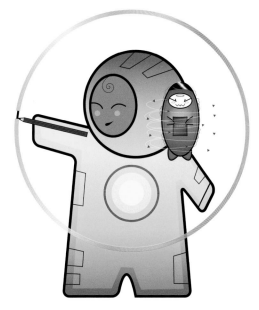

KINGFISHER

LONDON & NEW YORK

KINGFISHER
LONDON & NEW YORK

Text and design copyright © Toucan Books Ltd 2019
Illustrations copyright © Simon Basher 2019
www.basherbooks.com

Published in the United States by Kingfisher
175 Fifth Ave., New York, NY 10010
Kingfisher is an imprint of Macmillan Children's Books, London

Author: theCoderSchool
Consultants: Robin Ulster and James Denby
Editor: Anna Southgate
Designer: Leah Germann
Indexer: Marie Lorimer

Dedicated to Nathan Beasley

Distributed in the U.S. and Canada by Macmillan,
175 Fifth Ave., New York, NY 10010

Library of Congress Cataloging-in-Publication Data
has been applied for

ISBN 978-0-7534-7509-6 (Hardcover)
ISBN 978-0-7534-7510-2 (Paperback)

Kingfisher books are available for special promotions and premiums.
For details contact: Special Markets Department, Macmillan,
175 Fifth Ave., New York, NY 10010.

For more information, please visit www.kingfisherbooks.com

Printed in China

9 8 7 6 5 4 3 2 1
1TR/0519/WKT/UG/128MA

CONTENTS

INTRODUCTION

Coding is increasingly becoming a big part of our daily lives through the many smart devices we use. Every kid who learns to code will be that much better prepared for a successful future in whatever field he or she chooses. If you want to learn to code, you're in the right place. This book shows your how easy it is to use Scratch 3.0, a teaching platform and language released in 2019. An overview of the platform itself is followed by chapters introducing the fundamental concepts of coding and offering small applications (apps) that put them into practice. In later chapters you can test all that you've learned with a few more complex applications and build your first actual computer game. You'll also find a bunch of fun challenges to try along the way.

Why Scratch?

Scratch is developed by the Lifelong Kindergarten Group at the MIT Media Lab. It is available for free at https://scratch.mit.edu.

Scratch is the ideal teaching platform and language for anyone new to coding. With Scratch, coding is simplified so you can focus on the logic of the code and make fun apps really quickly. Scratch is great with graphics too, letting you code and control characters and objects more easily than most other languages. What better way to learn to code than by making cool, engaging apps?

What's theCoderSchool?

theCoderSchool is a cool and fun place for kids to learn how to code. Founded in 2014 and based smack in the heart of Silicon Valley, California, the school is growing fast with locations around the country. Its founders Hansel and Wayne wrote this book and they are honored to be sharing their experiences with you. You can find out more about them online, at www.thecoderschool.com.

SCRATCH BASICS

Itching to learn about Scratch? Let me be your guide. This cool programming language was invented by MIT Media Lab and is designed to help kids learn to code. The best thing about Scratch is that you can create programs just by draggin' n' droppin'. That's right, there is almost no typing at all! Take my mini tour of the program and you'll see how it works. I'll teach you all you need to know about sprites, command groups, and code blocks, and how to put them together.

YOUNG SCRATCH

I made my first appearance in 2003. In the early days, I was only available in desktop form, which means I had to be downloaded from the Internet and you couldn't use me online! This all changed in 2013 when I was ten years old. I was finally hooked up to the Internet and cut loose in The Cloud. All you needed to use me was a web browser, and I was ready to go.

As a teenager, in 2019, I was given a brand-new look, became more versatile, and even got a new name—Scratch 3.0. Not only am I easier to use now, but I can translate into other languages and work with a bigger range of physical devices. Best of all, I can play on a smartphone or a tablet.

1

In the Know:

The first Scratch project to be uploaded was called "Weekend." It used an earlier version of Scratch that didn't run in The Cloud. It was uploaded for others to download and run locally. It's a picture from a visit to Toscanini's ice-cream parlor in Cambridge, Massachusetts, and has clickable actions. You can still see it today at: https://scratch.mit.edu/projects/104/.

Mix It Up!

"Remixing" allows users to save a copy of someone else's code and change it to make it their own. Users have been able to make project modifications (a.k.a. mods) and remix code for a while now, but this feature has really taken off in the past few years. Take a look at the Scratch home page and you'll see some of the more popular remixed projects. (You can see how to do this for yourself on pages 48–49.)

BEGINNER'S GUIDE

Read through these pages to learn how to start Scratch and to find out about some of its basic functions. This will introduce you to the program and make it easier to learn from the activities in the rest of the book.

Getting Started

First, you need to know how to start Scratch. Open up a web browser and follow these steps. (Note that Scratch 3.0 does not support Internet Explorer.)

STEPS

1 Click in the address bar, and type in scratch.mit.edu.

2 In the upper-right-hand corner, use the Join and Sign-in buttons to get started. You don't have to join Scratch to code, but you'll need to join and sign in if you want to save the projects you create.

3 In the upper-left-hand corner you'll see the Scratch logo. Beside this is a button labeled Create. Click this to open the default Scratch screen.

The Scratch Screen

Your default screen should look like the image below. See the Code tab in the upper-left-hand corner. It's selected by default and is used when you want to build code. The notes below tell you what is happening in the different areas on your computer screen. You can refer back to this page when working through the chapters in this book.

Choose the command group you need. (See also page 14.)

Click the green flag to run your program.

Click the red stop sign to end your program.

This is the stage. You can watch your program run here.

Click here to grow or shrink your stage size.

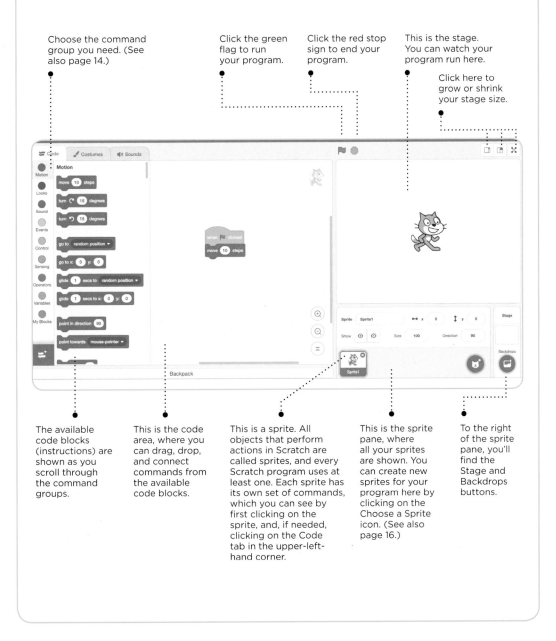

The available code blocks (instructions) are shown as you scroll through the command groups.

This is the code area, where you can drag, drop, and connect commands from the available code blocks.

This is a sprite. All objects that perform actions in Scratch are called sprites, and every Scratch program uses at least one. Each sprite has its own set of commands, which you can see by first clicking on the sprite, and, if needed, clicking on the Code tab in the upper-left-hand corner.

This is the sprite pane, where all your sprites are shown. You can create new sprites for your program here by clicking on the Choose a Sprite icon. (See also page 16.)

To the right of the sprite pane, you'll find the Stage and Backdrops buttons.

1

The Command Groups

When coding with Scratch, you use code blocks from different command groups. Each group is a different color depending on the type of command.

Motion

Looks

Sound

Events

Control

Sensing

Operators

Variables

My Blocks

Dark Blue: "Motion" commands control a sprite's movement—for example, how far and in what direction it moves.

Purple: "Looks" commands control appearance—for example, what a sprite looks like or what it says. They also control the background.

Violet: "Sound" commands control the different types of sounds that can be played.

Yellow: "Events" commands let you run code depending on an event, such as pressing a key. This is also where you will find the green flag coding block that is essential to almost all of your Scratch coding.

Light Orange: "Control" commands are for when a sprite needs to repeat an instruction, to wait before doing something, or to test for certain conditions.

Light Blue: "Sensing" commands detect whether a sprite is touching certain things, such as the mouse-pointer, an edge, or another sprite.

Light Green: "Operators" commands include comparing things and various math and text commands.

Dark Orange: "Variables" commands are for creating and using variables or lists.

Pink: "My Blocks" commands allow you to create new code blocks of your own.

Saving Your Work

Scratch autosaves at regular intervals. You can also use the File menu in the upper left of your screen to start, manage, and save your projects if you've signed in.

Working with Code

To code your sprites, just drag code blocks into the code area and connect them together. The order in which you connect them will be the order in which the instructions are run. To remove a code block from the code area, just drag it back over to the available commands. To undo a mistake, try Ctrl-z (or Cmd-z on a Mac). To test code, just click it.

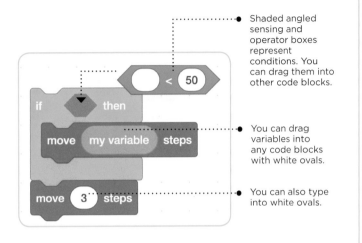

Shaded angled sensing and operator boxes represent conditions. You can drag them into other code blocks.

You can drag variables into any code blocks with white ovals.

You can also type into white ovals.

Extensions

Various "Extensions" allow you to use additional code blocks, such as playing musical instruments, translating text into many languages, and drawing with your sprites. Some of the projects in this book involve using musical instruments and drawing.

You'll find the blue Extension icon below the list of command groups.

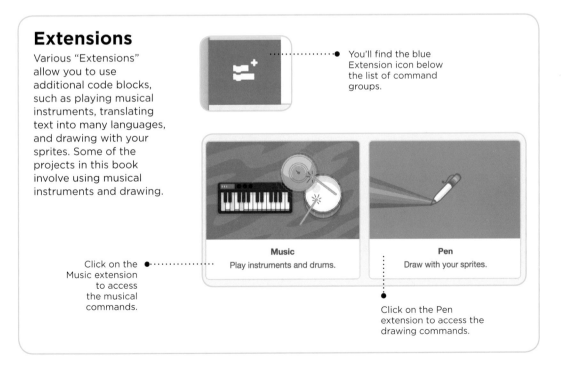

Music
Play instruments and drums.

Pen
Draw with your sprites.

Click on the Music extension to access the musical commands.

Click on the Pen extension to access the drawing commands.

BEGINNER'S GUIDE

The Sprite Pane

The sprite pane is where you'll find all your sprites. The basic information here includes name, position, size, and direction. You can create new sprites using a costume from the library, a costume you draw, a random costume, or one you upload.

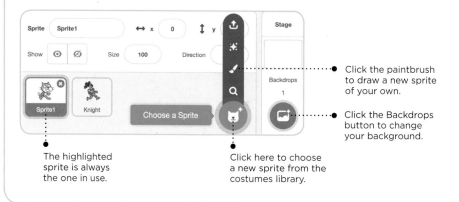

Click the paintbrush to draw a new sprite of your own.

Click the Backdrops button to change your background.

The highlighted sprite is always the one in use.

Click here to choose a new sprite from the costumes library.

Costumes

When a sprite is selected in the sprite pane, you'll see a Costumes tab in the top-left-hand corner of your screen. Click on this to access the drawing area below, where you can choose a costume from the library or use various tools to draw freehand and add text and color.

Name your costume here.

Choose a fill color here.

Choose a line color here.

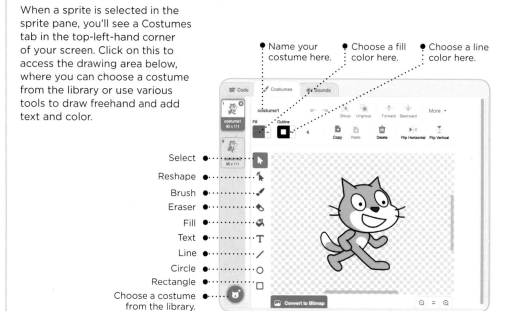

Select
Reshape
Brush
Eraser
Fill
Text
Line
Circle
Rectangle
Choose a costume from the library.

Backdrops

When the Stage button is clicked, you'll see a Backdrops tab in the top-left-hand corner of your screen. Click on this to access the drawing area, where you can change your background.

Name your backdrop here. •⋯⋯

Upload a backdrop from your camera. •⋯⋯

Upload a backdrop from your computer. •⋯⋯

Add a surprise backdrop. •⋯⋯

Draw your own backdrop. •⋯⋯

Choose a backdrop from the library. •⋯⋯

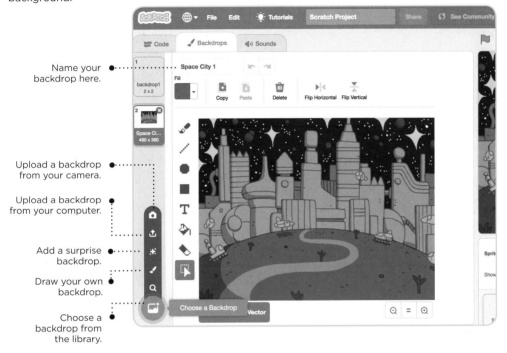

Sounds

When either the stage or a sprite is selected, you'll see a Sounds tab in the top-left-hand corner of your screen. This is where you can edit the sounds that you might use with your sprites.

PROGRAMMING

I'm all about creating instructions for a computer to perform. I make your mom's cell phone come to life and enable you to play games on your tablet. Computer programming is also called "coding," and Scratch has several tricks ("concepts" if you're a smarty-pants) that help smooth the way. Ever wondered what sequencing involves? Or creating loops and variables? Want to know how to use x and y coordinates? Check in with my Scratch programming team to find out.

SEQUENCING

In computer coding, all actions have to follow one another in an exact sequence, one at a time. All coding works this way. Think about getting dressed in the morning. If you don't pull on your socks before putting on your shoes, it just won't work. You will need to buy new socks, for starters!

Use my tricks to discover the importance of getting your code in the right order. Say you want a sprite to draw something. The sequence of your code will be the order in which your sprite completes its drawing. You will use sequencing every time you code.

2

TRY THIS!

Make the Scratch Cat draw a square one line at a time. After completing the square, make the Scratch Cat say "theCoderSchool is a cool place to learn to code!"

You'll find the drawing code blocks in the Pen extension group (see page 15).

Code Checker

Drag the code blocks into the code area and connect as shown. Click the green flag and test it out.

An "erase all" command clears any previous drawings.

FUN CHALLENGE

See if you can change the sequence to draw the square in the reverse direction. (Hint: Change the values in the "point in direction" code blocks and see what happens.) Turn to page 90 to see if you got it right.

Make the cat move in a clockwise direction.

Make the cat wait a second after each line.

Make the cat take 50 steps to draw each line.

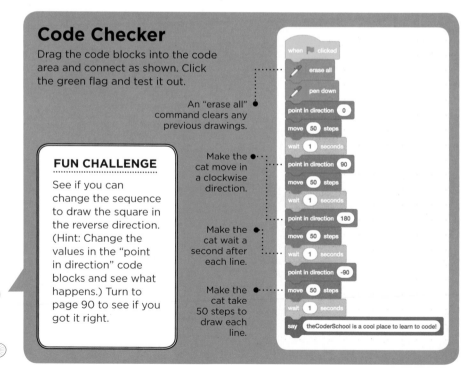

X AND Y COORDINATES

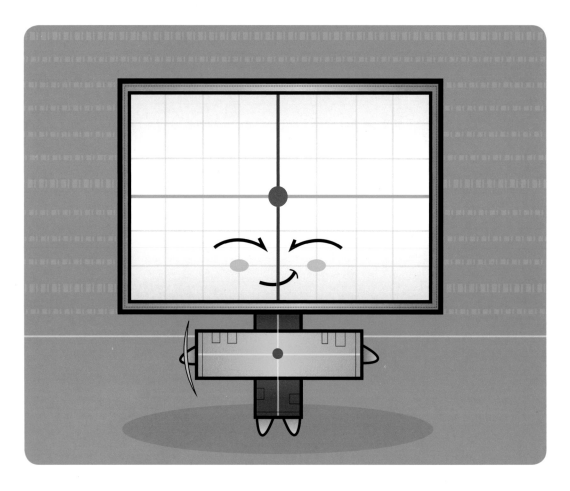

Where are we? If you know the answer, then you are on our level! That's right, we are the X and Y Coordinates that help to locate something on a grid. To do this, we use two imaginary lines called axes that cross at the center of the stage. The x coordinate determines horizontal location. Its range runs from the far left side of the stage to the far right. The y coordinate determines vertical location. Its range runs from top to bottom. Our axes cross at x = 0 and y = 0.

TRY THIS!

Make the Scratch Cat glide to the top-right-hand corner of the stage. Then have it go back to the center of the stage again.

Start by selecting the Xy-grid backdrop in the sprite pane.

Note that the stage is a 480 × 360 rectangle. The x position can range from –240 to 240 from left to right. The y position can range from 180 to –180 from top to bottom. This will help you decide which coordinates to plot.

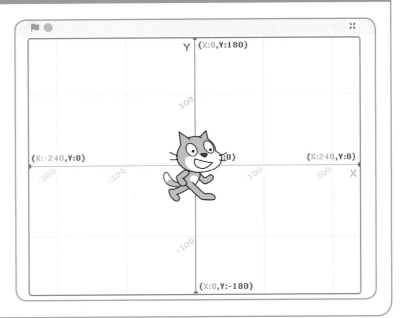

Code Checker

Drag the code blocks into the code area and connect as shown. Try clicking on the green flag now and watch the Scratch Cat glide across the stage.

Plot coordinates to make the cat glide to the top-right-hand corner of the stage.

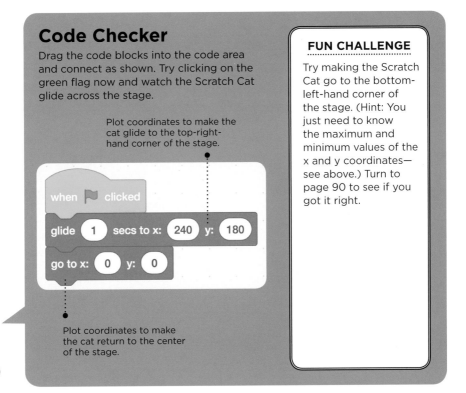

Plot coordinates to make the cat return to the center of the stage.

FUN CHALLENGE

Try making the Scratch Cat go to the bottom-left-hand corner of the stage. (Hint: You just need to know the maximum and minimum values of the x and y coordinates—see above.) Turn to page 90 to see if you got it right.

EVENT

Welcome to the main Event—that's me! I allow a program to perform actions based on certain "events" that occur. Events can be simple things such as mouse clicks or key presses, or complex things such as sprite collisions or receiving messages. Just think of any video game and consider all the events that need to be detected in order to make other actions occur—say, a missile has to hit a target to sink an enemy ship.

Back in the Scratch world, you can try your own hand at some "event-driven programming" by creating some code that involves pressing the right arrow key.

2

TRY THIS!

Make the Scratch Cat move 10 steps to the right each time you press the right arrow key.

This exercise teaches you how to create an event so that the program senses when a certain key is pressed.

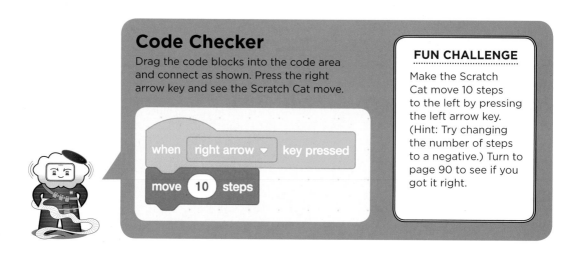

Code Checker

Drag the code blocks into the code area and connect as shown. Press the right arrow key and see the Scratch Cat move.

when [right arrow ▾] key pressed
move (10) steps

FUN CHALLENGE

Make the Scratch Cat move 10 steps to the left by pressing the left arrow key. (Hint: Try changing the number of steps to a negative.) Turn to page 90 to see if you got it right.

MULTISPRITE

I'm the concept that allows you to build something using more than one sprite. Once you find out how I work, you'll be dropping sprites into all your programs.

Try to think of a video game that doesn't have multiple sprites. Got one? No, I didn't think so—they are very rare. Instead, think of a game in which lots of sprites interact with each other. The key is knowing how to make this work and that's where I come in. I use my programming pal Event to trigger the actions of each sprite.

2

TRY THIS!

Choose two sprites and have them say "Hello" to each other—both at the same time, and for two seconds.

This exercise teaches you how to trigger multiple sets of code using the same event.

How it Works

For this exercise, it is essential that each sprite is given the right command.

STEPS

1 Click on the Choose a Sprite icon in the sprite pane to create a second sprite. We chose the beetle.

2 With the cat sprite selected in the sprite pane, click on the Code tab above the code area. Connect the cat's code blocks as shown.

3 Select the beetle sprite in the sprite pane. Repeat step 2 for the beetle, changing the message to "Hello Cat!"

4 Click on the green flag and watch your sprites say "Hello!" to each other.

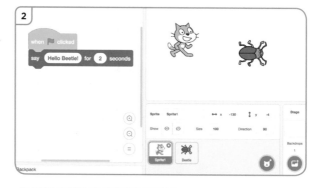

FUN CHALLENGE

Connect four sets of code to the same event, by adding two more sprites. This time, have one say hello after another. (Hint: Use the "wait" command from the Control command group.) Turn to page 91 to see if you got it right.

VARIABLE

My role is to act as a placeholder for information—a number, some text, or whatever—so that you can track that "value" as it changes.

Say you want to create a program that asks a person's name and says that name later. Since every user has a different name, that is the "value" that needs to change. Here's how I do it: First, you build code that makes me store whatever answer needs to be tracked. Then, when you want to use the answer, you just come to me—I always use the most recent answer stored. Neat, eh?

Making a Variable

When you start a new project in Scratch, you will find a ready-made variable, called "my variable" in the Variables command group.

To use the ready-made variable, you need to rename it. You can do this by right-clicking the "my variable" code block (Ctrl-click on a Mac). A pop-up window will appear in which you can change the name to whatever you need for your project.

You might want to use a variable for just one sprite. Click the Make a Variable button and a pop-up window will appear for naming the variable. There is also an option to use the variable "For all sprites" (the default) or "For this sprite only."

For other projects, you might want the variable to be visible in the stage area. If this is the case, check the box to the left of the variable once you have named it (see above).

TRY THIS!

Make the Scratch Cat ask "What's your name?" and then respond, "Hello...," saying the name.

This exercise teaches you how to create a variable to store a user's name. It also shows you how to add text to a variable using the join block in the Operators command group.

How it Works

You can use variables in lots of ways to make a program behave differently each time it is run.

STEPS

1 First make and name your variable. You can do this using the Make a Variable button in the Variables command group or by renaming "my variable" (see above).

2 Drag the code blocks into the code area and connect as shown.

3 To add the "answer" and "name" variables, drop them into the white ovals in the code blocks.

4 Click the green flag and test it out. Change your reponse to the question to see the variable in action.

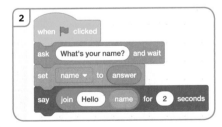

IF/THEN

I'm a concept with a fancy name: a boolean condition. Think of me as an if/then statement with only two possible outcomes, and you'll find me easier to understand. I'm all about testing to see if a condition is true or false and what to do about it. For example, "if" it is raining outside, "then" take an umbrella.

I can help you test lots of things, such as the value of a number. Say you want to create a program to check whether a number is odd or even. I can use a nifty "mod" command to find out the remainder when dividing a number by two. Using an "if/then/ else statement," I can then tell if the original number was odd or even.

TRY THIS!

Make the Scratch Cat ask the user to choose a number. When the user responds, the Scratch Cat will tell you whether the number is odd or even.

This exercise involves using an "if/then/else" condition to test whether the chosen number is even or odd.

Code Checker

Drag the code blocks into the code area and connect as shown. Click the green flag and test it out. Change the number a few times to see "if/then/else" in action.

The "mod" operator does the math. It works by dividing the chosen number by two. If the remainder is 0, then the number is even. If not, the number is odd. •

Find the "if/then/else statement" in the Control command group.

Place the "equals" command block first, then drop the "mod" command block into it. Drag and drop the variable "answer" into the "mod."

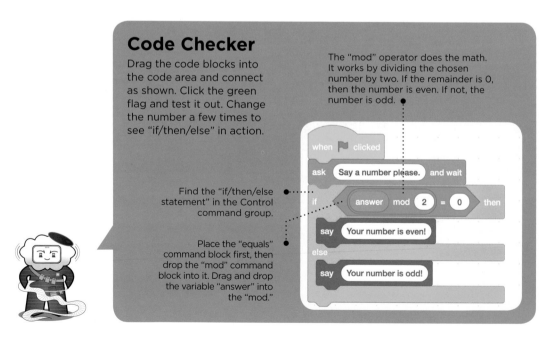

LOOP

I am, without doubt, the most dizzying concept of all. Some might even say that I'm loopy! I'm the programming concept to call on when you need to do something over and over again. Say you want to write a program in which something needs to happen 100 times. Instead of writing the same line of code 100 times, I can do it for you in an easier way. I work by using one code block that keeps on repeating anything within its loop until it has done this 100 times. It's a neat trick that allows you to write less code. Try me out and see how you like the shortcut.

2

TRY THIS!

Make the Scratch Cat count from 1 to 100, displaying each number for 0.1 seconds.

This exercise combines the "repeat" code block in the Control command group with a variable.

Code Checker

Drag the code blocks into the code area and connect as shown. Try clicking on the green flag now and watch the Scratch Cat count to 100!

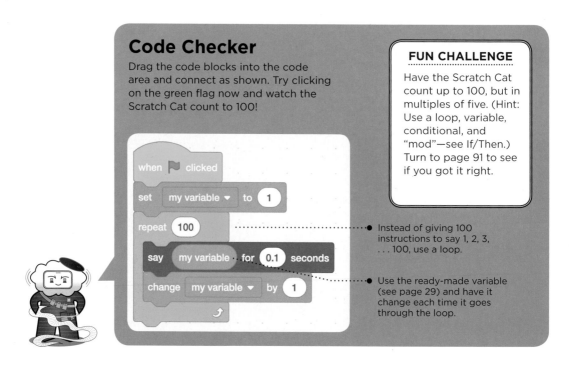

Instead of giving 100 instructions to say 1, 2, 3, . . . 100, use a loop.

Use the ready-made variable (see page 29) and have it change each time it goes through the loop.

FUN CHALLENGE

Have the Scratch Cat count up to 100, but in multiples of five. (Hint: Use a loop, variable, conditional, and "mod"—see If/Then.) Turn to page 91 to see if you got it right.

FUNCTION

I'm the kind of concept that lets you group any code that needs to be repeated.

Say you want to create a program that draws a circle. First, you need to know that a circle is made up of 360 degrees. Then you can use me to create a function that draws just one degree of a circle. Once I'm in place, I ask my buddy Loop to "call" this function 360 times. Hey presto! You've got a circle. Once you've defined your function, you can use it as many times as you want without having to retype any of its code.

TRY THIS!

Make the Scratch Cat draw a circle.

This exercise involves creating a function in order to group code that needs to be repeated.

How it Works

In Scratch, a function is called a Block. You can create one by using "Make a Block," in the My Blocks command group.

STEPS

1 Make a new Block. Call your Block "OneDegree." It will show up as a "define" block in the code area.

2 Now drag the code blocks into the code area and connect as shown. Click on the green flag and watch your sprite draw a perfect circle.

It is good practice to include the "pen up" command. Without it, a sprite continues to draw until you create a new project.

FUN CHALLENGE

Make the cat draw a second circle to create a figure eight. (Hint: Add a second function that goes in reverse and use a loop to call it 360 times.) Turn to page 92 to see if you got it right.

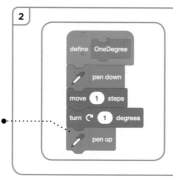

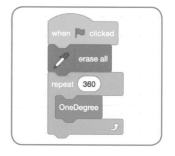

MINI APPS

Don't be fooled by the name. Sure, I have fewer lines of code than other software programs, but I pack a mighty punch in the coolness arena. I come in many different forms and allow you to test your basic coding skills before trying to write a complicated program. Mini apps use all the tools that you'll need for longer programs. It means you can get a whole load of practice in a fun and speedy way. Meet the apps and let them show you how they work.

THE MAGICIAN

They call me The Magician and I have a trick or two up my sleeve, I can tell you. If you like magic, you'll enjoy having fun with this mini app. In a simple case of now-you-see-it, now-you-don't, I can make a sprite disappear in front of your very eyes . . . and reappear in a completely different spot.

When it comes to programming, the disappearing act is actually perfected by Function, although Loop and the X and Y Coordinates have a role to play, too. Abracadabra, let's get started!

3

TRY THIS!

Make the Scratch Cat disappear from one part of the stage and reappear in another.

PROGRAMMING

You'll use the following concepts from Chapter 2:
• Sequencing
• X and Y Coordinates
• Loop
• Function

You'll also learn to:
• Set and change the size of a sprite using code blocks in the Looks command group.

Code Checker

Drag the code blocks into the code area and connect as shown. Click the green flag to make the Scratch Cat disappear . . . and reappear.

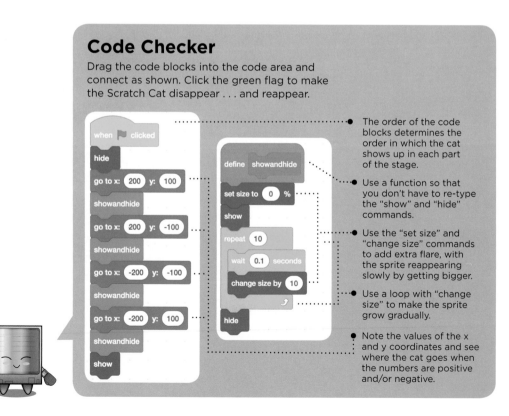

- The order of the code blocks determines the order in which the cat shows up in each part of the stage.

- Use a function so that you don't have to re-type the "show" and "hide" commands.

- Use the "set size" and "change size" commands to add extra flare, with the sprite reappearing slowly by getting bigger.

- Use a loop with "change size" to make the sprite grow gradually.

- Note the values of the x and y coordinates and see where the cat goes when the numbers are positive and/or negative.

WALKING SPRITE

Have you ever seen a sprite go walking? Well, you soon will, because that's just what I do. Remember meeting the X and Y Coordinates? I combine those guys with If/Then to show you how to make things wrap around a screen. Once you have the Scratch Cat walking from left to right and back around, you'll be able to repeat the trick with any other sprite you choose. It's a useful concept to master, as it is a feature of many video games.

Make the Scratch Cat walk from left to right and wrap around the stage.

PROGRAMMING

You'll use the following concepts from Chapter 2:
• Sequencing
• X and Y Coordinates
• Event
• If/Then

How It Works

Extra fun comes in changing the backdrop each time the Scratch Cat walks across the stage.

STEPS

1 Click on the Stage button in the sprite pane, and select the Backdrops tab. Add any two backdrops you like from the library.

2 Drag the code blocks into the code area and connect as shown. Press the right arrow button to try it out.

FUN CHALLENGE

Use the up and down arrow keys to make the sprite go up and down as well. (Hint: It is very similar to left and right, except you need to enter y coordinates.) Turn to page 92 to see if you got it right.

3

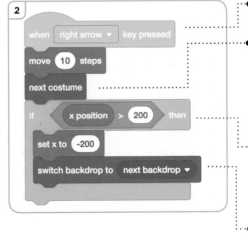

Use a "when key pressed" event to trigger movement.

Switching costume every 10 steps makes the cat look as if it's really walking. The sprite has two costumes by default, so you can switch back and forth.

Use an "if/then" command to make the cat switch to the opposite side of the stage when it gets close to the right-hand edge.

Use the "switch backdrop to next backdrop" command to give the cat a different background each time it wraps around the stage.

SPIRAL MAKER

Round and round and round I go! Take one look at me, and you'll be hypnotized for sure. Just watch as I start small in the middle and then circle round in a perfectly even spiral. This is such an easy trick, you'll have it mastered in no time.

Sure, the Scratch Cat draws me using a Pen command, but Loop and Variable are the true programming maestros behind my stunning form, and what a team they make. Pick a color and let's get drawing!

TRY THIS!

Make the Scratch Cat draw a spiral.

PROGRAMMING

You'll use the following concepts from Chapter 2:
- Sequencing
- Loop
- Variable

You'll also learn to:
- Draw using code blocks in the Pen extension group (see page 15).
- Increase a variable's value inside a loop.

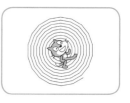

Code Checker

Drag the code blocks into the code area and connect as shown. Click on the green flag and watch the Scratch Cat draw.

Use a loop to repeat the same code over and over again.

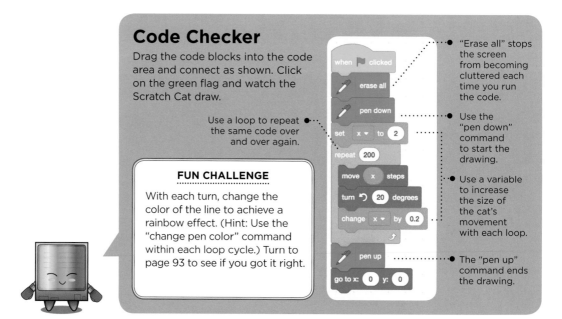

"Erase all" stops the screen from becoming cluttered each time you run the code.

Use the "pen down" command to start the drawing.

Use a variable to increase the size of the cat's movement with each loop.

The "pen up" command ends the drawing.

FUN CHALLENGE

With each turn, change the color of the line to achieve a rainbow effect. (Hint: Use the "change pen color" command within each loop cycle.) Turn to page 93 to see if you got it right.

TUNE MAKER

Finally an app where you get to make some noise . . . well, more of a tuneful song actually. I'm here to show you how to use Function to repeat musical phrases in a piece of music. I've chosen *Mary Had a Little Lamb*, but you can try any music you like.

It's with me that Sequencing really shines—your tune would sound lousy with all the notes out of order! Once you've played one merry ditty, you'll love experimenting with me and will have soundtracks for all your games in no time.

3

TRY THIS!

Play a pretty tune on the keyboard.

PROGRAMMING

You'll use the following concepts from Chapter 2:
• Sequencing
• Function

You'll also learn to:
• Choose the notes played on the keyboard using code blocks in the Music extension group (see page 15).

Code Checker

Drag the code blocks into the code area and connect as shown. Click on the green flag and listen to your music play.

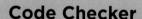

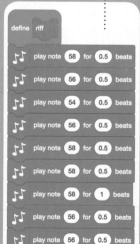

Using a function means you don't have to re-type the musical note commands.

Using the "play note" command allows you to choose the note you use. See how the notes are listed as numbers. When you click on the note number a pop-up shows you where it is on a keyboard. For example, 60 is a middle C note. The notes for Mary had a Little Lamb are: EDCDEEE; EDDDEGG; EDCDEEE; EDDEDC.

CHASING GAME

Set me up and watch a dopey dog sprite chase your mouse-pointer as you move it around the screen. Wherever your pointer goes, that sprite is sure to follow. It's a great function that's used in many games.

   I'm a big fan of If/Then and use two of those guys inside Loop. You'll soon get the hang of it. When you're playing, be sure to keep your eye on that sprite, because it might just catch up with you yet. Game over!

3

TRY THIS!

Have the Scratch Dog chase your pointer.

PROGRAMMING
You'll use the following concepts from Chapter 2:
• Sequencing
• If/Then
• Loop

You'll also use:
• A new sprite: Dog1.
• "Touching" in the Sensing command group.

Code Checker

Drag the code blocks into the code area and connect as shown. Click on the green flag to give the Scratch Dog the runaround.

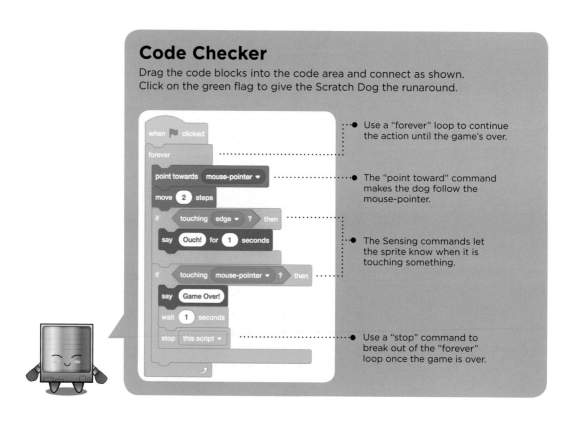

Use a "forever" loop to continue the action until the game's over.

The "point toward" command makes the dog follow the mouse-pointer.

The Sensing commands let the sprite know when it is touching something.

Use a "stop" command to break out of the "forever" loop once the game is over.

3D GHOST BOMBER

In this game, you use your mouse-pointer to touch things being thrown at you by a ghost. The more you touch, the higher you score. But, touch a bomb and you lose a life. Scared of ghosts? I'll help you swap it for something else. Games like this involve a lot of code, but with my sneaky ways, you can remix apps that already exist. It means you can customize games without having to start from scratch.

TRY THIS!

STEPS

1 Log in to your Scratch account and go to: https://scratch.mit.edu/projects/290964045/

2 Click on Scratch's REMIX option and save your own version.

3 With the ghost sprite selected, click on the costumes tab.

4 Click the Choose a Costume button to see the pop-up library of available costumes for your sprite.

5 Select a new costume and click on it so that it appears in your game.

6 Click the green flag to play and you should see your chosen costume instead of the ghost.

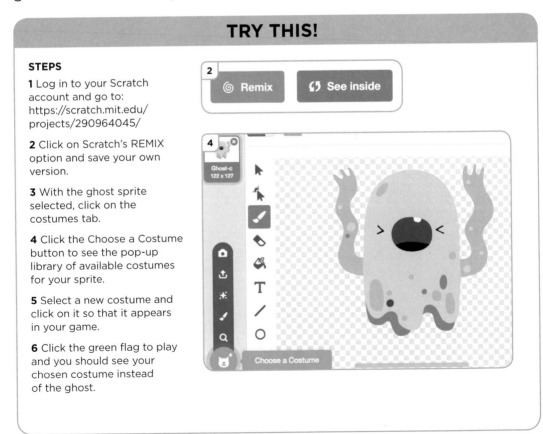

CHARACTER COUNTER

How many letters does it take to spell your name? Don't answer that, because I can tell you myself. It's a very simple trick, after all.

First, I make use of Sequencing (so that I know to ask what your name is before trying to count the characters). Then I use the "length" operator block to help me count the characters. It's a foolproof combo that lets me get it right every time, even if your name happens to be Rumpelstiltskin. I'm useful whenever you need to work with strings of characters, because you'll often want to know how many you have in total.

3

TRY THIS!

Have the Scratch Cat tell you the number of letters in your name.

PROGRAMMING
You'll use the following concepts from Chapter 2:
• Sequencing
• Variable

You'll also learn to:
• Use commands inside commands by placing the "join" code block twice, one within the other.
• Use the "length" code block, which can tell you how many letters are in a variable.

Both are in the Operators command group.

Code Checker
Drag the code blocks into the code area and connect as shown. Click on the green flag to set the Scratch Cat in action.

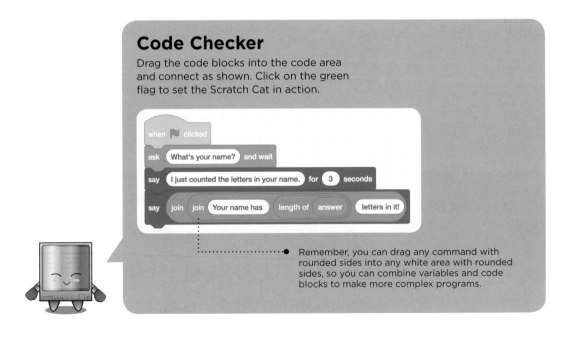

Remember, you can drag any command with rounded sides into any white area with rounded sides, so you can combine variables and code blocks to make more complex programs.

CHALLENGE APPS

All programming languages use logic and that includes Scratch! It means getting characters such as Variable, Loop, and If/Then involved. Of course, you know about those guys already, but they have a bunch of cool friends that they want you to meet: Shape Drawer, Cat Jumper, Dodgeball, Racecar Game, and Number Sorter. These smart types will test what you've learned so far and will really put your logic skills into action. Are you up to it?

SHAPE DRAWER

4

What do you know about geometry? Well, a polygon is any shape that has a set number of sides and the same number of corners. A "regular" polygon is a shape where all the sides are the same length—for example, a square. It means that the angles inside the corners are all the same size, too. I'm going to show you how to write a function (in Scratch, "Make a Block") that lets the user pick a number so that the Scratch Cat then draws a regular polygon with that many sides.

TRY THIS!

Make the Scratch Cat ask "How many sides?" When the user responds with a number—say, 5—make the cat draw a regular polygon with five sides. The program divides the number of sides into 360 (the total number of degrees in a polygon) to give the number of degrees by which the cat needs to turn at each corner. Be careful, if you draw too many sides, there may not be enough room on the stage!

PROGRAMMING

You'll use the following programming concepts from Chapter 2:

- Sequencing
- Event
- X and Y Coordinates
- Loop
- Function

Setting Up

First you need to make your function using the Make a Block button in the My Blocks command group. Always give a function a name that makes sense. You also need to click on the Add an input button and add an input called "sides" (see right). Inputs are values that functions need in order to process or calculate results.

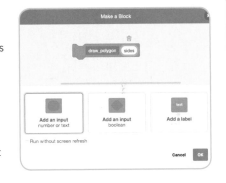

WORKING THE CODE

Drag the code blocks into the code area and connect as shown. Click the green flag to make the Scratch Cat ask the question.

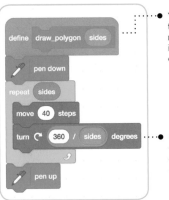

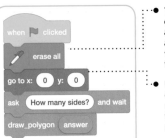

You can drag the "sides" number input into the other code blocks.

Use a simple Operator command to do the math.

The "erase all" command clears any results from a previous game when the green flag is clicked.

Use x and y coordinates to return the cat to the middle of the screen each time.

Use the new "draw_polygon" function that allows the user to choose the number of sides they want their polygon to have.

4

CAT JUMPER

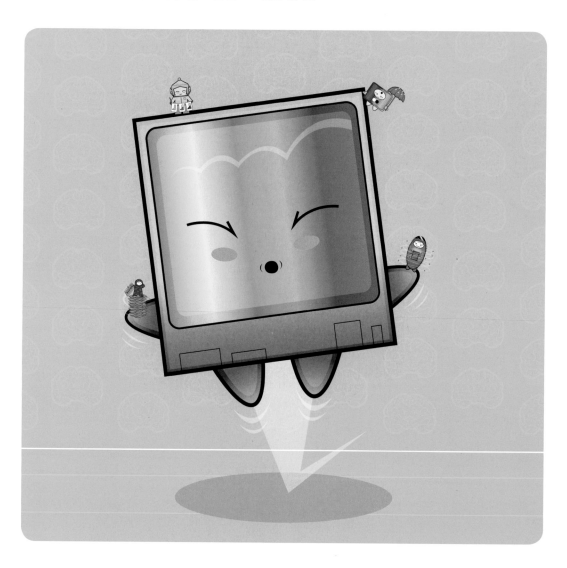

4

Lots of video games involve a sprite jumping: jumping onto enemies, jumping onto walls, jumping over bad guys, you name it. Using the basic concepts you have learned already, let's see if you can get the Scratch Cat jumping! Once Variable has set how high the cat jumps, you can use Sequencing, Loop, and If/Then to have that jumping cat bouncing all over the screen.

Make the Scratch Cat jump up in the air.

PROGRAMMING

You'll use the following concepts from Chapter 2:
• Sequencing
• Loop
• X and Y Coordinates
• If/Then

Take the Challenge

Drag the following code blocks to the code area, step by step, and see if you can fill in the blanks here and there.

STEPS

1 First, initialize the app by moving the cat to the center of the screen and set the "fallspeed." This is a variable that determines how fast the Scratch Cat falls.

2 Now connect a "forever" loop containing two "if/then" statements. These will check for user input and then act on it. In this case, the action depends on which key the user presses. Here's your first challenge: Add code to the empty "if/then" statements so that the Scratch Cat moves left 10 steps when the left arrow is pressed and moves right 10 steps when the right arrow is pressed.

3 Now, to give the Scratch Cat some gravity, drop these code blocks inside the "forever" loop, right at the bottom. This makes the cat look as if it gains speed as it falls. The "fallspeed" becomes more negative with each loop, so changing the cat's y position and making it appear to fall faster and faster.

4 To give the Scratch Cat jumping power, add an "if-spacebar-is-pressed" condition. Drop it inside the "forever" loop, again right at the bottom. Here's your second challenge: See how the fallspeed is a negative number when the cat is falling? What could you set the fallspeed to, in order to make the cat jump? Try a few numbers and see what happens.

5 To make your game more realistic, you need a "floor." This code will make sure the cat stays at y = 0 (the floor), if we try to set it to less than 0 in the code above. Drag this section of code into the "forever" loop too, at the bottom.

You can find the full code on page 93. Take a look and see if you got it right.

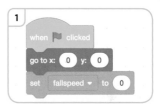

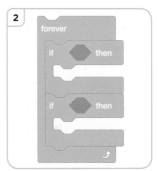

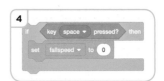

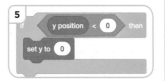

4

DODGEBALL

Quick, run! Up! No, down! *Ouch!* Who doesn't love a game of dodgeball? My version uses separate controls so that two people can go head-to-head with each other. In terms of programming, Multisprite allows you to have a different sprite for each player as well as the balls, while the X and Y Coordinates set up the play area for you. My code looks complicated, but it is really very simple. Better still, it's pretty much two sets of the same instructions, so you can tell yourself it's only half the work!

4

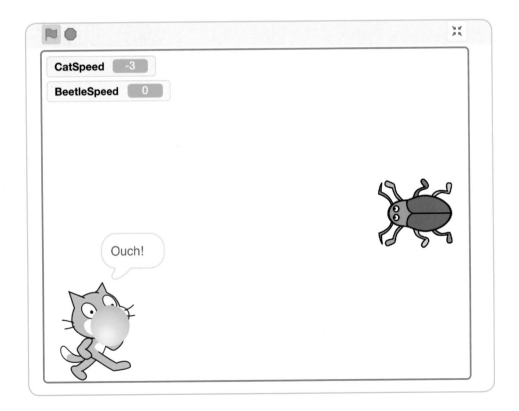

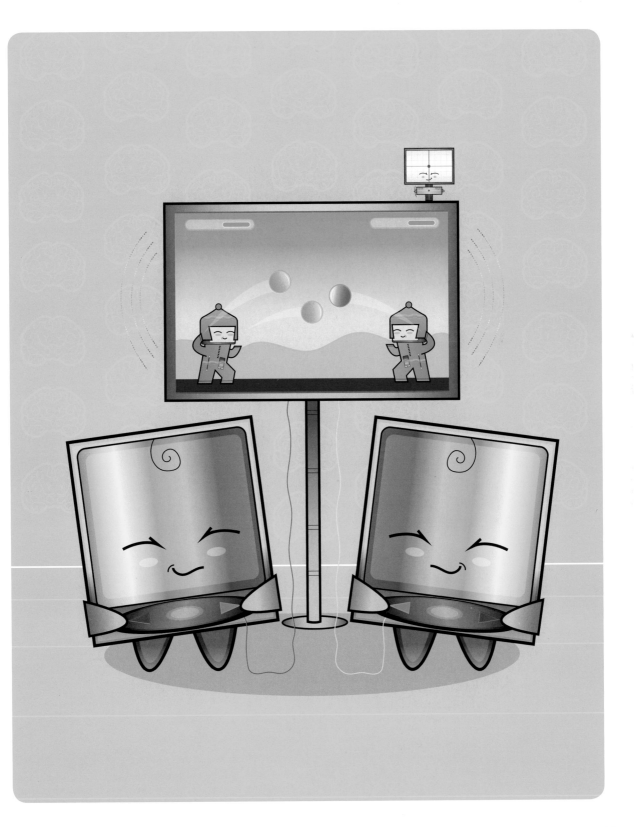

DODGEBALL

TRY THIS!

Create a two-player game of dodgeball.

PROGRAMMING

You'll use the following concepts from Chapter 2:
• Sequencing
• Event
• X and Y Coordinates
• Multisprite
• Loop
• Variable
• If/Then

You'll also use:
Cloning

Setting Up

1 Click on the Choose a Sprite icon in the sprite pane to create three new sprites: the Beetle and two Balls.

2 Click on the Cat sprite and rename the sprite "Cat." Repeat to rename the other sprites Beetle, CatBall, and BeetleBall.

4

The Cat and the Beetle

In this game, one player operates the cat and the other operates the beetle. Each player can control the sprite's movement and shoot unlimited balls at the other player!

WORKING THE CODE

Work the code for the cat (left) and the beetle (right), with the right sprite selected in the sprite pane. A useful shortcut is to drag the code from your cat onto the icon for your beetle and change as necessary.

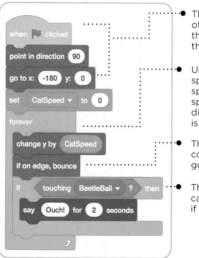

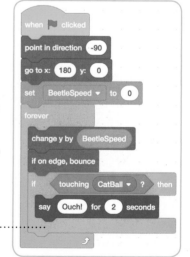

The first three lines of code "initialize" the sprites—they get them ready to start.

Use a loop to keep each sprite in motion. Using a speed variable keeps the sprite moving in the same direction until another key is pressed.

The "if on edge, bounce" code stops the sprite from going off the screen.

The "touching" code causes a sprite to react if hit by a ball.

Note that the cat and beetle have similar codes.

Sprite Movement

Set up each sprite's movement separately. The cat code is on the left and beetle code on the right.

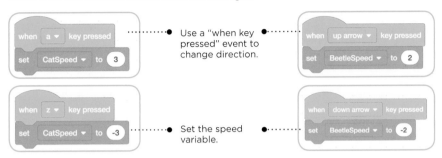

Use a "when key pressed" event to change direction.

Set the speed variable.

Cloning the Balls

This is where you use the "clone" command to make lots of balls for the cat and the beetle to keep throwing at one another. The code under "when I start as a clone" is run by every clone that gets created.

WORKING THE CODE

The catball code is on the left and beetleball code on the right. Make sure you have the correct ball sprite selected in the sprite pane each time you create new code. Drag the code blocks to the code area and connect as shown.

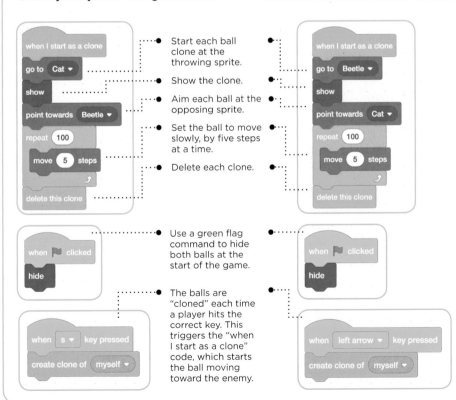

Start each ball clone at the throwing sprite.

Show the clone.

Aim each ball at the opposing sprite.

Set the ball to move slowly, by five steps at a time.

Delete each clone.

Use a green flag command to hide both balls at the start of the game.

The balls are "cloned" each time a player hits the correct key. This triggers the "when I start as a clone" code, which starts the ball moving toward the enemy.

RACETRACK GAME

Ready to race? You'd better be! I'm a game that pits you against the machine. See how well you can play against a computer. I'm a challenge app that shows you how to create an artificially intelligent (AI) opponent to take on as you zoom around the racetrack. I use Loop to keep you going round and round, while If/Then lets you know when you bump into the edge of the racetrack. Sorry, what's that? What racetrack? Well, it's the one you are about to paint . . .

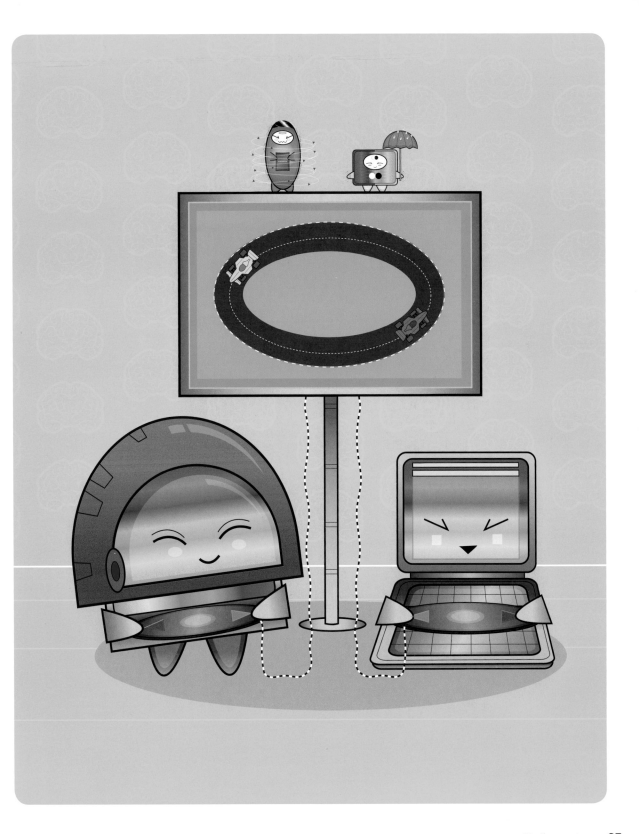

RACETRACK GAME

TRY THIS!

Create your own racecar game.

PROGRAMMING

You'll use the following concepts from Chapter 2:
- Sequencing
- X and Y Coordinates
- Event
- Multisprite
- Variable
- If/Then
- Loop

You'll also use:
- Sensing
- Messaging
- Basic Artificial Intelligence (AI)

4

Setting Up the Track

STEPS

1 First draw your racetrack. Click the Stage button to the right of the sprite pane and select the Backdrops tab in the top-left-hand corner of your screen.

2 Select the Rectangle tool to the left of the drawing area, choose a light blue (or any similar color), and fill the screen entirely.

3 Select the Brush tool, change the brush size to 150, and draw an oval track in yellow. Leave some light blue around the entire outside area of the track.

4 Select Fill, choose a dark blue, and fill in the inside of the track.

5 Finally, select the Line tool, and draw a red line—the finish line!

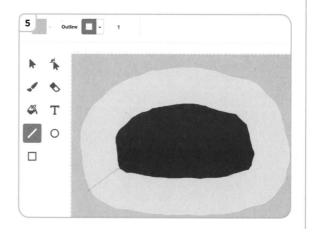

The Scratch Cat

First, you'll need to adjust the size of the cat so that it can fit on the racetrack. You can do this using the "Size" option in the sprite pane. Then, enter the cat's code.

Change the cat's size from 100 to 30 in the sprite pane.

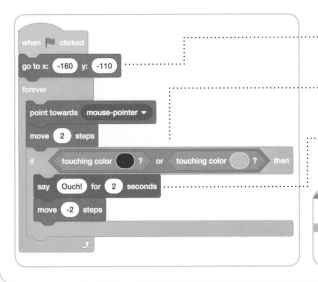

WORKING THE CODE

Use the coordinates to place the cat just in front of the red finish line on your track. You may need to adjust the numbers for the track you have drawn.

Use an "if/then" statement to check two conditions at the same time—whether the cat is touching one or the other color (see below).

When the cat touches the inside or outside of the track, it says "Ouch!" and backs up a few steps.

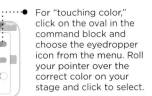

For "touching color," click on the oval in the command block and choose the eyedropper icon from the menu. Roll your pointer over the correct color on your stage and click to select.

4

The Scratch Bat

Add a second sprite to the sprite pane (we chose the bat), and set its size to 20%. Then enter the bat's code below.

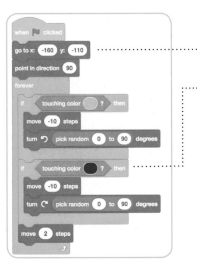

WORKING THE CODE

As with the cat, note where the coordinates place your bat and adjust to make sure it starts just in front of the finish line.

The reason you paint the inside of the track a different color to the outside is because the AI bat needs to know what direction to turn in. It goes forward until it hits either the inside color or the outside color. If the bat hits the inside color, it knows it needs to turn right to keep going. That's why it backs up a few steps and turns right a random amount between 0 degrees and 90 degrees before moving on. Same goes for the outside track—but turning left instead!

RACETRACK GAME

Who Wins?

You need to keep adding to the cat and bat code so that the computer knows which one crosses the line first.

WORKING THE CODE

Make sure you have the correct sprite selected in the sprite pane each time you add new code. The cat code is top right, the bat code bottom right. Create a second "if/then" statement for each as shown below and drag them into the cat and bat codes—at the bottom of their forever loop.

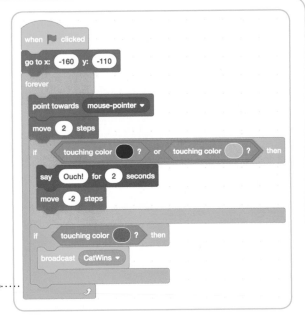

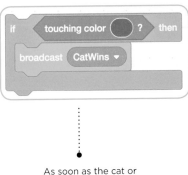

As soon as the cat or bat touches the red finish line, the winning message is broadcast. Broadcast is a command block that lets you type in any message and broadcast it to everyone.

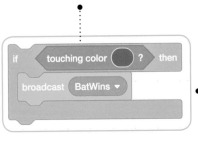

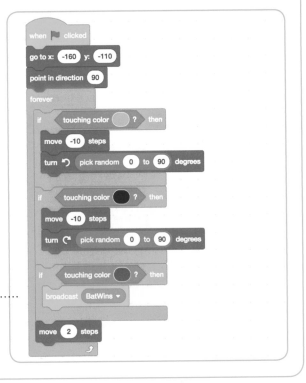

4

Finishing Touches

1 Create some end screens. Select the Stage button to the right of the sprite pane and select the Backdrops tab in the top-left-hand corner of your screen. Right-click (or ctrl-click on a Mac) your racetrack backdrop and choose duplicate.

2 Select the Text tool at the left of the drawing area, choose white as your color, and type "Cat Wins!" inside the track.

3 Duplicate another backdrop, and repeat the above step and type "Bat Wins!" inside the track.

4 Next you need to add code to receive the message that says a sprite has won. Add this code to the code area on the stage. The logic is easy—if you get a message saying "Cat Wins!," you change the backdrop to Backdrop2, and then stop all code. Now that you get it, add the code for "Bat Wins" too, in the same code area.

5 Finally, to make sure you reset (initialize) the backdrop when you start racing, add code so that when the green flag is clicked, the stage's backdrop is set to the Backdrop1.

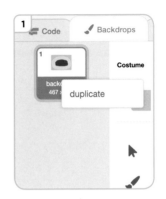

4

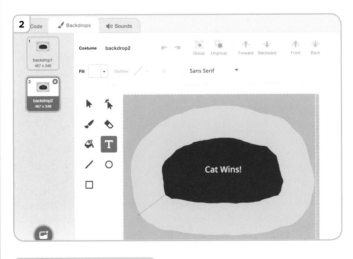

NUMBER SORTER

I'm an advanced concept, so watch out!
I love playing with numbers and want to
show you a "sorting algorithm." An algorithm
is a fancy way of saying a process has to be
followed in a certain order to get something
done. In this exercise, I'll show you how to
build an "Insertion Sort," one of the simpler
sorting algorithms. The stars of this program
are Variable, Loop, and If/Then. But there's
another critter who wants to play: List.

4

TRY THIS!

Write a program to make the
Scratch Cat sort numbers for
you. The code relies on creating
two variables: a normal variable
and a list variable. The code
allows a user to enter random
numbers, which the Scratch Cat
puts in numerical order from
lowest to highest.

PROGRAMMING

You'll use the following concepts
from Chapter 2:
• Sequencing
• Loop
• Variable
• If/Then

You'll also use:
• A "list" variable to hold the
numbers you'll be sorting
• An "if this OR that, then"
condition

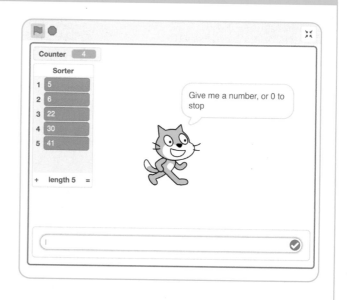

NUMBER SORTER

Take the Challenge

See if you can complete some of the steps for yourself in this activity.

STEPS

1 Start by creating two kinds of variables: a "variable" named Counter and a "list variable" named Sorter. Both can be found in the Variables command group.

The Counter keeps track of the numbers being checked.

The Sorter holds the numbers once sorted.

Be sure to check the box to the left of the "counter" and "sorter" variables, as shown. This makes both visible while the cat does its sorting.

2 Build the code as shown. "Delete all from sorter" clears any numbers from a previous game. The "forever" loop keeps the Scratch Cat asking for numbers, until the user enters "0." Can you figure out what goes in the "if" statement here? (Hint: What does the user need to enter to make the cat stop? You'll need an Operator command and a Sensing command; see page 93 if you need help.)

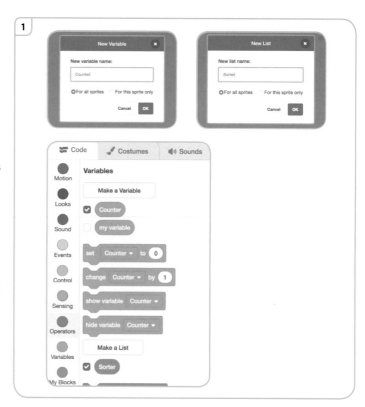

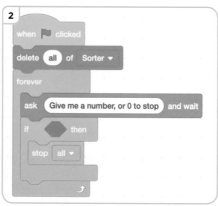

4

3 Drag the next two code blocks into the "forever" loop in step 2, connecting them immediately below the "if/then" statement. The first sets the Counter to 1 so that the program sorts numbers from the first one entered. The second inserts every new number at position number 1 of the Sorter list.

4 Try it out. You'll see that the numbers enter the Sorter in the order in which you give them. You'll also see that the Counter is not actually counting yet.

5 To get the Counter to count, insert this "repeat until" loop between the two code blocks you added in step 3. Run the code again and you can see that the Counter now counts, but the numbers are not being sorted.

6 Try changing the "repeat until" condition as shown. This should make the Counter work through the numbers given so far, stopping once it finds the right spot for the latest number entered. But, instead, the Counter just keeps on counting. So what can the problem be?

7 The answer is that you need both "repeat until" conditions. (Hint: You can combine them by using a third Operator block: an "or" condition.) Drop this into the "repeat until" loop first and then see if you can work out where to put the conditions from steps 4 and 5.

8 If you get it right, you will see that the numbers appear in the sorter in numerical order, and the counter tells you the position of each new number—that is, the point at which it stopped counting.

You'll find the full code on page 93. See if you got it right.

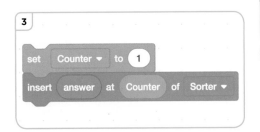

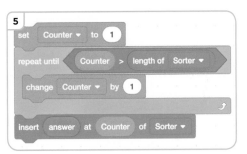

4

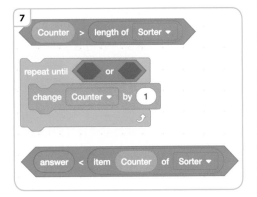

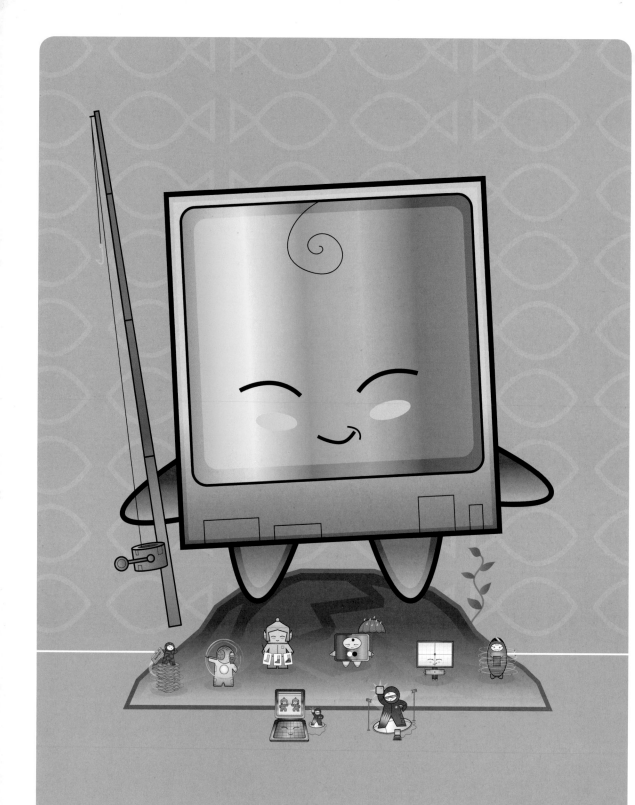

MEGA APP

So, you've completed all your training activities and have tried them out with a few apps and challenges. Think you're ready to build a computer game? I do . . . with a little help from me, that is. I have a mega app for you to try, an old favorite called Fish Food. Led by Sequencing, most of those smart characters from the Programming chapter have a role to play here, so expect to see a few familiar faces. You'll have some cool sounds to add, too.

FISH FOOD

Most video games have a main character and in this case it's called the Player Fish. Whoever plays your game (probably you) presses keys to help that critter navigate around the ocean. Its only job is to avoid hitting the big enemy fish while seeking out the little enemy fish. If the Player Fish bumps into a smaller fish, it chomps it down and grows bigger. But colliding with a bigger fish is not so good. When that happens, the Player Fish gets eaten. Hey, it's not all bad—it means you get to play the game again!

Step by step

You need to complete the following coding modules for this game to work properly. You will need to build them in the correct order so follow the steps carefully. Use my live version for reference at: https://scratch.mit.edu/projects/278144731/editor

5

Time 47

Setting Up

Start by creating the Player Fish. For this game, the fish needs two costumes—one for regular play and one for when it wins a game.

STEPS

1 Select the Scratch Cat sprite in the sprite pane and click on the Costumes tab in the top-left-hand corner of your screen.

2 Click on the Choose a Costume option and select the Fish-a sprite costume in the Animals category.

3 Repeat Step 2 to add the Party Hat-a costume in the Fashions category.

4 Remove the two Scratch Cat costumes by selecting each in turn and clicking on the "x" in the top-right-hand corner. You should only have the Fish-a and Party Hat-a costumes now.

5 With Sprite1 selected in the sprite pane, click on the Sounds tab in the top-left-hand corner of the screen. Use the Choose a Sound option to add two sounds: "Bubbles" and "Eggs."

6 Still with Sprite1 selected in the sprite pane, update the sprite name to Player. The name text field sits just above your sprites. This is now the Player Fish.

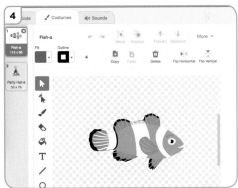

5

FISH FOOD

1: THE PLAYER FISH

Movement

The next step is to give the Player Fish the ability to move in all directions. Click on the Player Fish in the sprite pane, then select the Code tab.

PROGRAMMING

You'll use the following concepts from Chapter 2:
• Sequencing
• X and Y Coordinates
• Event
• If/Then
• Loop

You'll also use:
• Rotation styles
• Key pressing

WORKING THE CODE

Drag the code blocks to the code area and connect as shown.

Switch your sprite's costume to Fish-a and show it. This ensures a new game always starts with the right costume.

You can control how a sprite rotates. In this case, the Player Fish rotates "left–right."

Use a "forever" loop to enable you to move the Player Fish at all times by pressing certain keys.

Inside the loop, "if/then" instructions check for the "key pressed" events.

You are using your x and y coordinate knowledge to move the Player Fish by 2 in each direction depending on the key pressed.

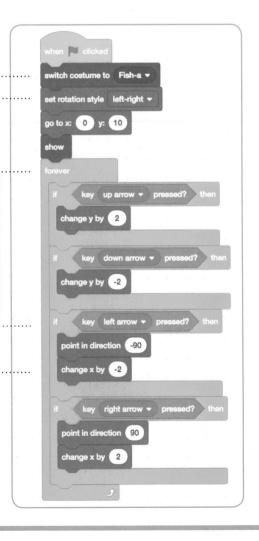

Growth

Now you need to enable the Player Fish to grow in size as it eats other fish. To do this, you need to set, or initialize, two variables: "playerAlive" and "playerSize."

PROGRAMMING

You'll be using the concepts from Chapter 2:
- Sequencing
- Event
- Variable
- If/Then
- Loop

You'll also use:
- Setting size
- Messaging

WORKING THE CODE

Drag the code blocks to the code area and connect as shown.

Defaults

Scratch variables start off with a default value, so make sure to change them if needed. For example, all sprites will start off at 100% in size. If your game requires a bigger or smaller sprite, change its size by updating the sprite pane.

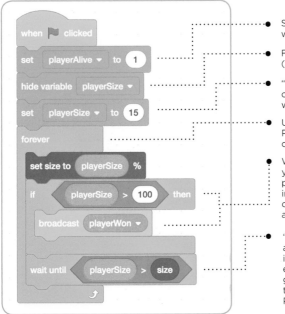

Set your variable so that each game starts with the Player Fish alive (1 is alive; 0 is dead).

For this game you want to "hide" the variable ("show" is the default).

"Set size" determines what percentage of the original costume the fish should be shown at when the game starts.

Use a "forever" loop to continually reset the Player Fish's size so that it can grow as it eats other fish.

When the Player Fish reaches 100% in size, you get to broadcast the message that the player has won. Simply type this message into the code-block window. "Broadcast" commands are often used to trigger actions and events in other sprites.

"Size" is the current size of the Player Fish at any point in the game. The playerSize variable increases each time the Player Fish eats an enemy fish. Each time the playerSize variable gets bigger than "size," then "size" increases to match it. And when "size" increases, the Player Fish grows on the screen.

5

FISH FOOD

1: THE PLAYER FISH

When the Player Fish Loses

Remember that the Player Fish can only eat enemy fish that are smaller than itself. If it tries to eat a bigger fish, the Player Fish dies and the game is over.

PROGRAMMING

You'll use the following concepts from Chapter 2:
• Sequencing
• Event
• Variable
• Loop

You'll also use:
• Messaging
• Rotation styles
• Sounds
• Changing effects

5

WORKING THE CODE

Drag the code blocks to the code area and connect as shown.

Messages

When you type in a new message for broadcasting and receiving, it gets stored. It means you only need to type each message once—after that it pops up as an option.

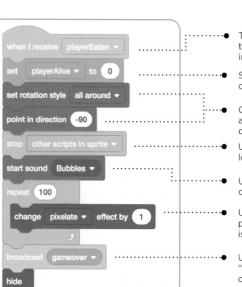

The "playerEaten" message is broadcast by the enemy fish when the Player Fish bumps into a larger fish.

Set your variable so that the Player Fish is dead (1 is alive; 0 is dead).

Change the rotation style to "all around," with a –90 direction to make the fish turn upside down and look dead.

Use the "stop" command to prevent a "forever" loop continuing to run for another sprite.

Use the Bubbles sound to signal the end of the game.

Use a "repeat 100" loop with the "change pixelate" to make the Player Fish look as if it is dissolving.

Use a new custom message to broadcast "gameover." This tells all the other pieces of code that the game has ended.

When the Player Fish wins

If you play well and the Player Fish eats all the smaller enemy fish without being eaten itself, you could win the game. The Player Fish starts out at 15% of its original size, and keeps growing until it reaches its full size at 100%. At that point, the game ends. You can adjust this percentage to make the game easier or more difficult to win.

Order of events

When the Player Fish disappears at the end of a game, it makes room for the game stats to pop up (see page 87).

PROGRAMMING

You'll use the following concepts from Chapter 2:
• Sequencing
• Event
• Variable
• Loop

You'll also use:
• Messaging
• Changing effects
• Sounds

5

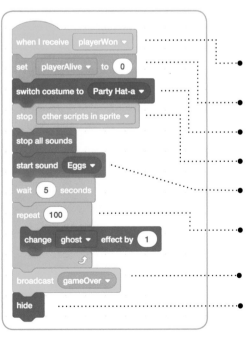

WORKING THE CODE

Drag the code blocks to the code area and connect as shown.

● The "receive" command in Events, triggered when the size of the Player Fish reaches 100%, sets the winning actions in motion.

● Set the "playerAlive" variable to 0. This signals that the game is over because you've won.

● Switch the sprite's costume to Party Hat-a to signal a celebration.

● Use the "stop" command to stop all code running in other sprites while this sprite's code continues.

● Play the Eggs sound to signal a celebration.

● Use a "repeat 100" loop to make the Player Fish disappear slowly.

● A "broadcast" triggers the final statistics to be displayed such as size and how many fish eaten.

● The "hide" command makes the Player Fish disappear.

FISH FOOD

2: THE ENEMY FISH

Setting Up

The next step is to create the other fish in the game—the enemy fish! This is a two-stage process. First you make a new sprite, then you create a second costume for that sprite.

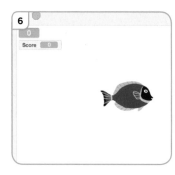

STEPS

1 To make the new sprite, select Choose a Sprite in the sprite pane. Select Fish from the Animals category.

2 Click on the Costumes tab in the top-left-hand corner of the screen, and delete Fish-a and Fish-d.

3 Select the Sounds tab with either Fish-b or Fish-c selected since both have access to the same sounds. Use the Choose a Sound option to add the Chomp sound.

4 With the Fish sprite selected in the sprite pane, create a variable "**For this sprite only**" and call it "enemySize," so that each clone will have its own size.

5 Create two more variables called: "fishEaten" and "score." When you make each variable check the box to the left to make them "show" in the Scratch screen.

6 In the Scratch screen, right click (Ctrl-click on a Mac) on the "fishEaten" and "score" variables and set both of these variables to "large readout" mode.

Movement

Just as you gave the Player Fish the ability to move, you now want to give the enemy fish some movement.

PROGRAMMING

You'll use the following concepts from Chapter 2:
- Sequencing
- Event
- Variable
- Loop

You'll also use:
- Rotation styles
- Random options

WORKING THE CODE

Drag the code blocks to the code area and connect as shown.

Show Variable

Remember variables have defaults (see page 77). Another way to make a variable "show" or "hide" is to check the box next to the variable when you create it (see step 5 on page 80).

5

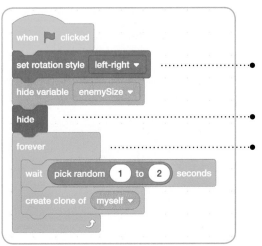

Set the rotation style as "left–right" to match the Player Fish.

"Hide" the variable so it doesn't show on the screen.

Use a "forever" loop to clone the fish, with a delay of either 1 or 2 seconds each time. You achieve this by using "pick random" in the Operators command group. This code creates a new clone of the enemy fish every 1 or 2 seconds.

FISH FOOD

2: THE ENEMY FISH

Cloning

You need to vary the size of the clones so that some are small enough to eat, while others are big enough to be afraid of. To make the game more fun, the enemy fish colors are randomly selected for each clone that's made.

PROGRAMMING

You'll use the following concepts from Chapter 2:
- Sequencing
- X and Y Coordinates
- Variable
- If/Then/Else

You'll also use:
- Cloning
- Random options
- Changing effects
- Gliding

Linking Events

Notice that "when I start as a clone" can be used multiple times in the program. This means that different actions can be triggered to run at the same time.

WORKING THE CODE

With the Fish sprite selected in the sprite pane, drag the code blocks to the code area and connect as shown.

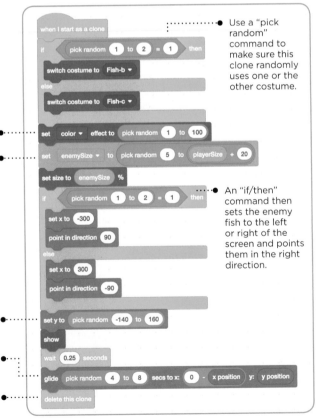

Use a "pick random" command to make sure this clone randomly uses one or the other costume.

"Set color effect" to use a random color each time an enemy fish is cloned.

Use variables to make the enemy fish randomly bigger or smaller than the Player Fish. Place the green operator blocks exactly as shown, and erase or overwrite any default figures in the white ovals.

An "if/then" command then sets the enemy fish to the left or right of the screen and points them in the right direction.

Another "pick random" command determines where each clone starts on the y axis.

The "glide" command makes the fish move across the screen.

The clone is deleted on reaching the other side.

5

Touching and Eating

This section of code determines what happens when one of the cloned enemy fish touches the Player Fish. If the cloned fish is bigger, it eats the Player Fish. If the cloned fish is smaller, you want to hear a Chomp sound and see the Player Fish increase in size.

PROGRAMMING

You'll use the following concepts from Chapter 2:
• Sequencing
• Variable
• If/Then/Else

You'll also use:
• Cloning
• Sensing
• Sounds
• Messaging

WORKING THE CODE

Drag the code blocks to the code area of the Fish sprite and connect as shown.

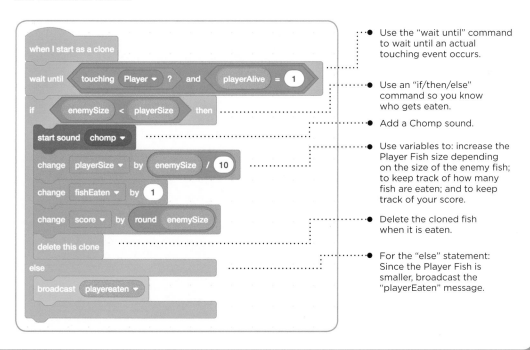

Use the "wait until" command to wait until an actual touching event occurs.

Use an "if/then/else" command so you know who gets eaten.

Add a Chomp sound.

Use variables to: increase the Player Fish size depending on the size of the enemy fish; to keep track of how many fish are eaten; and to keep track of your score.

Delete the cloned fish when it is eaten.

For the "else" statement: Since the Player Fish is smaller, broadcast the "playerEaten" message.

FISH FOOD

3: THE BACKDROP

Setting Up

A backdrop is easy to add, but makes so much difference to
your finished video game. Let's give your fish some ocean
to swim in and choose some music to play.

PROGRAMMING

You'll use the following concepts
from Chapter 2:
• Sequencing
• Event
• Variable
• Loop

You'll also use:
• Changing effects

STEPS

1 Select the Stage button to the
right of the sprite pane. Click
on the Choose a Backdrop icon.
Select the Underwater 1 backdrop
from the Underwater category.

2 With the Stage button still
selected, click on the Sounds tab
in the top-left-hand corner of the
screen. Select and add Dance
Magic from the Loops category.

3 Create a variable called "time."
Check the box that makes it visible
on the Scratch screen and set
the variable to display in "large
readout" mode (see page 80).

WORKING THE CODE

With the Stage button selected, drag the code
blocks to the code area and connect as shown.

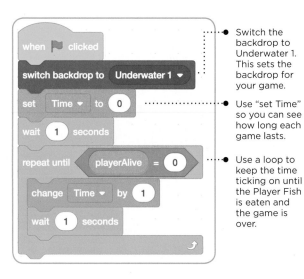

Switch the
backdrop to
Underwater 1.
This sets the
backdrop for
your game.

Use "set Time"
so you can see
how long each
game lasts.

Use a loop to
keep the time
ticking on until
the Player Fish
is eaten and
the game is
over.

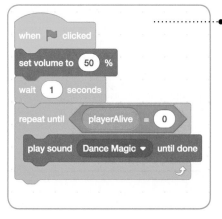

Create a
second code
block with a
loop so that
music plays
until the game
is over.

Setting Up

To finish the video game, you want to tell the player how they did: How many fish they ate; how long they played for; and whether they won or lost. The messages will pop up on the Scratch screen at the end of the game. To do this, you'll create a third sprite whose job it is to display all these messages. You'll also create a fourth sprite called "Timer." This sprite's job is to keep track and display the time so the player knows how long they played.

STEPS

1 In the sprite pane, select the Paint icon and name the new sprite "Message."

2 Create Costume1, to look like our example. This is the screen the player sees when they lose the game. Use the Rectangle tool to the left of the drawing area to make the box for the scores. Use the Text tool to type in the text—choose any font you like at the top of the drawing area.

3 Right-click (Ctrl on a Mac) on Costume1 and choose duplicate to create Costume2, which will be your winning screen. Make it similar to our example, so that the box for the scores appears in the same location on the Scratch screen for both costume images.

4 Back in the sprite pane, select the Paint option to create another new sprite. This time call your new sprite "Timer." You want to create a new sprite whose sole purpose is to be your timer and will always be shown whether the player wins or loses.

5 Now create a costume for Timer, making it similar to our example.

5

FISH FOOD

4: GAME ENDS

Message Popups

When the Player Fish disappears at the end of the game, it makes room for your messages to pop up. This section of code determines where they will appear on the Scratch screen.

STEPS

1 With the Message sprite selected, create a variable called "sizeCategory" for all sprites and check its little box to the left so it's displayed. Set it to "large readout" in the Scratch screen.

2 On the Scratch screen (where the action happens), drag your variables—"fishEaten," "score," "sizeCategory," and "time"—to their appropriate places, so they line up with the message you made in step 1. (Note that you may have to switch your variable back to "normal readout" in order to do this. Be sure to return to "large readout" afterward—see page 80.)

3 With the Timer sprite selected, click the Code tab and drag the code blocks to the code area, connecting them as shown. This makes up one simple command to position your timer in the bottom-left-hand corner of the screen.

5

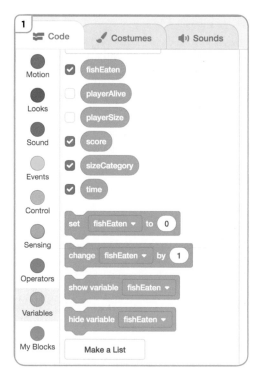

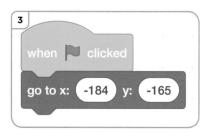

The Stats

So that all the statistics show up at the end of the game, you need your Time, fishEaten, sizeCategory, and Score variables to start counting from the start of the game. Then, at the end of the game, the computer can tell the player how well (or badly) they have done. You could add these variables in any sprite since they are global. We chose to add them into our "Message" sprite so that they would be in one central location.

WORKING THE CODE

With the Message sprite selected in the sprite pane, drag the code blocks to the code area and connect as shown.

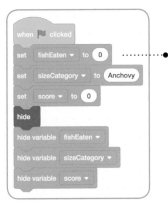

Use "set" commands to set and initialize your variables. Then hide the message itself using the "hide" command. Hide the variables as well.

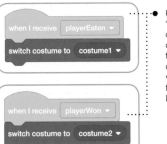

Use the "switch costume" command to set your costumes for when your fish wins or loses.

PROGRAMMING

You'll use the following concepts from Chapter 2:
• Sequencing
• Event
• Variable
• If/Then/Else

You'll also use:
• Changing effects

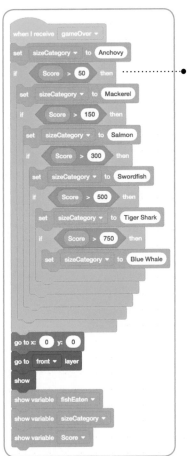

A series of "if/then" statements determines the Player Fish's final size. The bigger the fish, the better the player did in the game.

5

FUN CHALLENGES: THE SOLUTIONS

Got a problem? Call me and I'll give you the solution. Remember all those fun challenges that were set in the earlier chapters? Well I've got the answers for you right here. You'll have tried these out yourself already, so let's see if you got them right. And don't worry if you didn't—all the key points are explained in the following pages, which means you'll know for next time. And with better understanding comes better coding. Ready to get down to business?

THE SOLUTIONS

Page 20: Sequencing

THE CHALLENGE:

To see if you are able to change the sequence so that the Scratch Cat draws the square in the reverse direction.

● The key is to enter the "point in direction" figures in the reverse order.

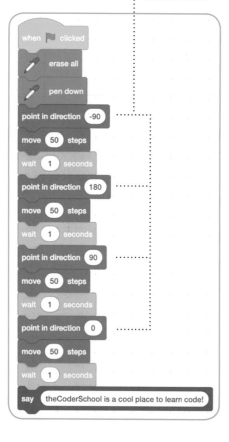

Page 23: X and Y Coordinates

THE CHALLENGE:

To see if you can make the Scratch Cat go to the bottom left-hand corner of the stage.

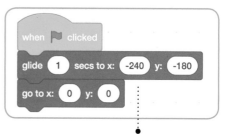

The key is to enter the coordinates for the bottom-left-hand corner of the stage. You just need to know the maximum and minimum values of the x and y coordinates (x = –240 and y = –180).

Page 24: Event

THE CHALLENGE:

To see if you can make the sprite move 10 steps to the left when the left arrow key is pressed.

● First you need to trigger the event by pressing the left arrow key.

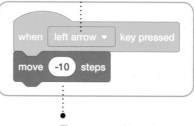

Then you need to enter a negative number for the steps to be taken.

6

Page 26: Multisprite

THE CHALLENGE:

To see if you can add two more sprites and have them say "Hello," too. You also want them to say "Hello" one after another rather than at the same time.

Add two more sprites and make sure you have the correct sprite selected in the sprite pane when you build each set of code.

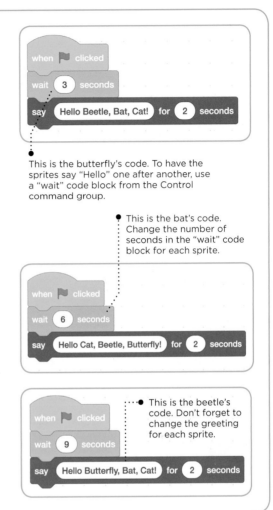

This is the butterfly's code. To have the sprites say "Hello" one after another, use a "wait" code block from the Control command group.

This is the bat's code. Change the number of seconds in the "wait" code block for each sprite.

This is the beetle's code. Don't forget to change the greeting for each sprite.

6

Page 32: Loop

THE CHALLENGE:

To see if you can make the Scratch Cat count up to 100, but in multiples of five. For this challenge, you need to add an "if/ then" loop inside the repeat loop.

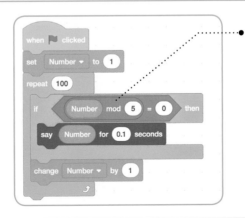

Drop a "mod" command inside the "if/then" loop (see page 30). This Operator command does the math. The "mod" command divides one number by another number and gives you the remainder. If the result is a zero, then you know the first number is divisible by the other.

THE SOLUTIONS

Page 34: Function

THE CHALLENGE:

To see if you can make the Scratch Cat draw a second circle after completing the first. It should be above the first circle, to complete a figure eight. For this challenge, one solution is to create a second function and call it 360 times.

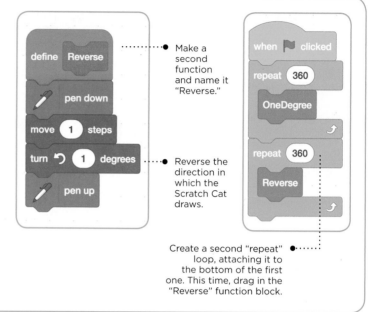

•···· Make a second function and name it "Reverse."

•···· Reverse the direction in which the Scratch Cat draws.

Create a second "repeat" loop, attaching it to the bottom of the first one. This time, drag in the "Reverse" function block. ···•

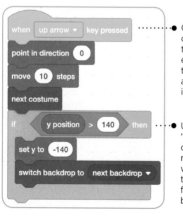

6

Page 41: Walking Sprite

THE CHALLENGE:

To see if you can use the up and down arrow keys to have the sprite go up and down as well. Achieving this is very similar to making the cat walk left and right, but this time you need to enter y coordinates instead.

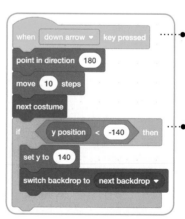

•···· Create code to trigger an event when the up arrow key is pressed.

•···· Use an "if/then" command to make the cat wrap around the screen from top to bottom.

•···· Create code to trigger an event when the down arrow key is pressed.

•···· Use an "if/then" command to make the cat wrap around the screen from bottom to top.

Page 42: Spiral Maker

THE CHALLENGE:
To see if you can change the color of the line with each movement the Scratch Cat makes, to give the spiral a very cool rainbow effect.

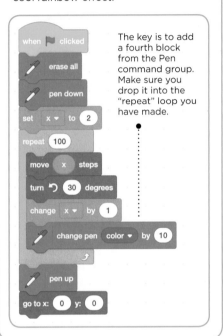

The key is to add a fourth block from the Pen command group. Make sure you drop it into the "repeat" loop you have made.

Page 57: Cat Jumper

CHALLENGE 1: To see if you can make the sprite move 10 steps to the left when the left arrow key is pressed and 10 steps to the right when the right arrow is pressed.

CHALLENGE 2: To figure out what value "fallspeed" should have to make the cat jump.

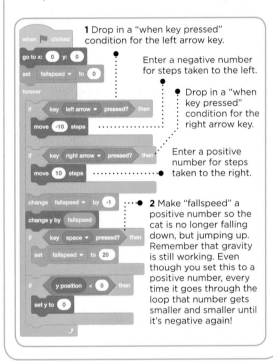

1 Drop in a "when key pressed" condition for the left arrow key.

Enter a negative number for steps taken to the left.

Drop in a "when key pressed" condition for the right arrow key.

Enter a positive number for steps taken to the right.

2 Make "fallspeed" a positive number so the cat is no longer falling down, but jumping up. Remember that gravity is still working. Even though you set this to a positive number, every time it goes through the loop that number gets smaller and smaller until it's negative again!

6

Page 71: Number Sorter

CHALLENGE 1: To add a condition to stop the program when the user enters 0.

CHALLENGE 2: To use a third operator that allows you to check two conditions.

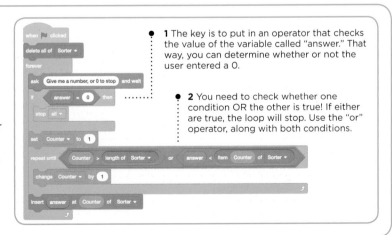

1 The key is to put in an operator that checks the value of the variable called "answer." That way, you can determine whether or not the user entered a 0.

2 You need to check whether one condition OR the other is true! If either are true, the loop will stop. Use the "or" operator, along with both conditions.

GLOSSARY

Algorithm A set of rules to be followed in calculations or other problem-solving operations, especially when done by a computer.

Angle Measured in degrees, this is the space between two intersecting lines at the point at which they meet.

App An abbreviation for the word "application," which is any software program written for any hardware platform.

Axis (plural axes) A fixed reference line for the measurement of coordinates.

Background The image of the stage that shows up behind the sprites.

Boolean condition An expression that is used to show one of two values being either true or false.

Broadcast In Scratch, this means to send a message to all the other sprites. It's a useful form of communication that enables certain code to be triggered by other events.

Clone A Scratch feature that allows a sprite to duplicate itself while the project is running. It is identical to its parent sprite. This is an extremely valuable feature in building many video game applications.

Cloud, The Where Scratch and your Scratch projects typically reside—out in the Internet rather than locally on your computer. Your computer links up with this through a network connection.

Code block Any instruction that can be dragged and dropped into the code area. Stacks of code blocks make up a script. The script makes a project able to run.

Command group Scratch code blocks are organized into different "command" categories, such as Motion, Sensing, Operators, Events.

Concept A fundamental rule, idea, or plan that can be used when trying to code a program.

Coordinates The x and y values that represent horizontal and vertical positions along their axes. These help you be able to code and control sprites at precise positions on the screen.

Costume The look and appearance of a sprite. Each sprite can have multiple costumes.

Customize When you take an example or sample of code and change it to be your own version, making it unique to yourself.

Default The initial value of something unless you change it. For example, if you create a variable, its initial/default value will be zero unless changed by you.

Degree A measurement of an angle so that a full rotation making a circle is 360 degrees.

Desktop A term commonly used to describe a computer that was not made to be mobile. These are larger systems with separate larger monitors in general, compared with a laptop, which is portable.

Drag n' drop Refers to how Scratch works, where the user can drag a command block out and drop it onto the code area to code. This system greatly reduces the need to type.

Geometry The area of mathematics that deals with points, lines, shapes, space, and how they relate with one another.

Green flag The button that is always used to start your programs running. It's green which means Go!

Initialize When you create your variables, you also want to initialize them, which involves giving them a first value to start off with.

Logic A particular way of thinking, especially one that is reasonable, well structured, and helps solves problems.

Nested When you have one loop within another loop.

Paint editor Scratch's built-in image editor.

Pixelate When an image is divided into its individual pixels.

Polygon A shape made with a minimum of three straight lines, called sides.

Popup A graphical display area, usually a small window, that suddenly appears in the foreground on your computer screen.

Quadrant Any of the four regions of a plane that has been divided by the x and y axes of a coordinate system.

Random When something is decided or picked by chance rather than by plan, purpose, or pattern.

Remixing One of Scratch's most useful features, it allows a user to take another project and make changes to/remix it, to make a new version for themselves.

Sensing A command group where the code blocks are used to detect something, such as when a sprite touches a certain color or comes into contact with another sprite or object.

Smart phone A cell phone integrated with a computer so that it has an operating system, web browser, and the ability to run software programs.

Software A collection of instructions that tell the computer what actions to perform.

Sprite In Scratch, any object that performs actions and functions controlled by scripts and code blocks.

Sprite pane The area within the Scratch screen where all the sprites from one project can easily be accessed, inspected, and updated.

Statistics A branch of mathematics that deals with collection, analysis, and interpretation of numerical data in large quantities for the purpose of making better decisions.

Syntax The spelling and grammar of a computer language. Computers are very rigid in what they can understand so when you code, it must be in the exact format that the computer can understand. This expected format is the syntax.

Tablet A mobile computing device that is flat and rectangular, similar to a magazine or pad of paper. They are generally controlled by a touch screen.

Web browser A software application that allows users to locate, access, and display web pages.

x-position The position of a sprite or the mouse along the horizontal axis.

y-position The position of a sprite or the mouse along the vertical axis.

INDEX